St Philip Neri

Nihil Obstat

Andreas Moore, L.C.L., Censor Deputatis.

Imprimatur

E. Morragh Bernard, Vic. Gen.

Westmonasterii, die 21a Februarii, 1958

St Philip Neri

A Portrait

Louis Bouyer

Translated by Michael Day

First published in English by Geoffrey Chapman in 1958

This edition first published in 1995

Gracewing
Fowler Wright Books,
Southern Avenue, Leominster
Herefordshire, HR6 0QF

ISBN 0 85244 299 8

CONTENTS

PREFACE TO THE
SECOND ENGLISH EDITION

IT WAS SAID OF ST PHILIP NERI THAT HE DREW people to himself as iron is drawn to a magnet. He had that attractiveness which the Holy Spirit bestows; making someone lovable, and at the same time inspiring the love of others in them.

The Congregation which grew up spontaneously around him had no special rule but only that charity which showed itself in care for the sick and the pilgrims to Rome and that formation in prayer from which the *Oratory* takes its name. There was to be that freedom among the members which would recall the early days of the Church when all were 'of one mind and one heart'. Baronius described it as 'a kind of well-ordered republic', for the followers of St Philip voluntarily accept to live the consequences of the religious life in community, without the vows of religion: 'Love is his bond, he knows no other fetter.'[1] This particular characteristic attracted John Henry Newman, who saw

1 Hymn to St Philip by Cardinal Newman.

that it was the natural development of the community life which he had lived with his friends at Littlemore. His establishment of the English Oratory at Maryvale in 1848 was the impetus for the modern growth of the Congregation.

There are now three Oratories in England, six in North America, besides houses throughout Europe and South America, and a foundation in South Africa. Each house is self-governing under its own provost, grouped in a confederation numbering some seventy-five in all.

The fourth centenary of St Philip's death occurs in 1995 and it is to be hoped that his influence together with that of his followers, including the Venerable John Henry Newman, may draw many to give themselves to serve their brethren in love, based on that heart-felt prayer to the God who has so loved us.

The Oratory
Edgbaston
1995

PROLOGUE

IT IS LATE AFTERNOON IN A ROMAN PIAZZA; THE heat is still oppressive and the roofs of the great white palaces stand out against a pitilessly clear sky. A few clumps of trees on the slope of Monte Pincio and the fifteenth-century façade of Trinita dei Monti rise up in the distance. The crystal plumes of a fountain wave lazily above the urchins splashing about in the basin and their voices ring out through the rainbow-coloured shower with the sharpness and clarity of everything here.

The siesta is over and already the tradeswomen are welcoming their first evening customers, tempting them with flowers, huge lemons from Naples and juicy water melons.

A fine lady hastens towards the Via Guilia in her carriage with its flashing ornaments and tinkling bells; she cares nothing for all this; but a young Monsignor on his way to the Roman College, his purple robes obviously new, looks as though he might be tempted were it not for the fact that he must maintain his dignity. Not so the noisy youths surging in twos and threes from the banks, shops and schools, or from the alleys where they have been dreaming the hot afternoon away in the shade of some convenient doorway.

The urchins, tempted from the fountain by this bustle, are still grubby but so radiant under their soaking rags and their shocks of tousled hair that in answer to their shrill entreaties one cheerfully casts a coin or two into their eager little paws.

But whatever is this strange procession that presses on through a barrage of laughter? Why is this handsome and well-dressed young man looking embarrassed, and what on earth is he carrying so gingerly in his arms? It is a fat and amiable retriever, wearing a ridiculous pink ribbon round its neck! A group of young men in holiday attire, scatterbrains, judging by their unrestrained laughter and buffoonery, follow him; in their midst we see, to our surprise, an aged priest who is obviously their leader. But is he really so old? True, his hair and beard are silver-white, but his face is as smooth as that of a child, and his vivid eyes, glancing swiftly from one to another, seem to communicate to all his unchanging happiness.

People call out to him from the crowd and he never tires of answering with a joke or a familiar wave of his delicate hand. He has a ready smile for everyone, a smile that has something personal about it for each. An urchin who suddenly presses his dirty but beaming little face against him receives a friendly flick of the hand which is as much a cuff as a caress.

We follow the happy band into a bookshop. The proprietor hurries forward with the latest theological works, to be greeted by the old man with more good-humour than enthusiasm. But wait a moment, isn't that a newly published collection of Dominican hymns? The group, scattered among the bookshelves, gathers again at once and an improvised choir joins the Father in singing a few lines by Fra Serafino Razzi.

They move on once more and now meet an entirely different figure, a Franciscan in a threadbare habit, his face behind his beard one suspects is lined by fasting, and his bare feet are lacerated with cuts. He is carrying a heavy wallet on his back and on his shoulder a small keg of wine.

The company seem in no way put out by his

appearance, on the contrary they welcome him as an old friend. 'How is it that you haven't been burnt at the stake yet, you old heretic?' calls out the priest, as soon as he catches sight of him. 'And how is it that they haven't yet put you on the rack?' replies the friar, keeping a straight face.

The banter continues and then the friar seems to have offered some sort of challenge to the old man, for he seizes the keg and to the delight of the bystanders drinks off a bumper from the bung-hole. Following this he hands back the keg, and, as if in recompense, takes off his hat and places it on the friar's head. The latter, without more ado, continues on his way amid a chorus of laughter, and the gay band makes off in the direction of the Tiber.

Everything is quiet now. They have entered the shade of a church where Vespers are just finishing; it is the church of Sant'Agnese on the Piazza Navona, and all the young madcaps chant the Psalms as gravely as if they were monks.

Not so long afterwards however, when they have reassembled, this time in the Father's room, they will be making such a deafening uproar that another priest, wearing the same white collar over his plain cassock, will thrust a frightened face through the half-open door. He won't say anything, the Father is no longer there, but he knows where to find him and the shadow of his huge form is seen slowly mounting the spiral staircase which opens suddenly on to a loggia on the roof.

'Father,' he says, faltering like a shy and sulky child, 'you can hear them from here. How do you think I can work with that row going on?' An affectionate laugh accompanies the reply 'Is it as bad as that! As far as I'm concerned, so long as they keep free from sin, they can chop wood on my back if they feel like it.' The learned Baronius goes down again grumbling; he has given in but is not very convinced.

The old man's limpid gaze rests tenderly on the horizon which every moment seems to grow more transparent; the sun sinks down behind the Janiculum where the sea breeze is beginning to stir the clustered trees. To the right one can see the flower of a vast newly built dome still surrounded by scaffolding.

11

A light which owes nothing to the clear and tranquil evening suffuses this marvellous face, alternately so old and so young as to appear ageless. But his solitude cannot last long. One by one the young men, serious now, yet still smiling, slip up by the narrow stairway and before long—one scarcely knows how—he is the centre of the group again.

Enthralled by so much peace and by the twilight still hesitating on night's threshold, they gather together silently, like children grouped around their father.

Suddenly the bells ring out over the Eternal City for the Angelus, one by one from the huge bell of the Lateran to the tinkling chimes of Santa Maria Maggiore.

Before going down and out into the night, as if to vanquish evil spirits, their voices are joined again in the Hail Mary.

They have all gone. Philip remains alone and the Holy Spirit, who has been his constant companion all through the day, takes possession of him in tranquillity.

I.—LAYMAN

WHENCE CAME THIS STRANGE ROMAN SOCRATES, this attractive saint from another more childlike world?

Philip Neri was born in Florence on the 21st July 1515, in the same year as Marignan[1] and St. Teresa. The waters of baptism had flowed upon him in the 'bel San Giovanni' so tenderly recalled by the exiled Dante. A Florentine, the son of a Florentine, no matter how much of a Roman he was later to become, he always kept, like some lingering perfume, the unmistakable fragrance of his native city.

His father seems to have squandered the entire fortune which Lucrezia da Mosciano brought to their marriage as her dowry, and it had been a large sum despite the fact that she was only the daughter of a carpenter. This is not to say that Francesco Neri, a wealthy notary, was a rake. The passion which held him in thrall was the

1 now Melegnano—the battle in which Francis I defeated the Swiss allies of Milan.

philosophers' stone. His young wife did not live very long and Philip knew only his stepmother, with whom he got on very well, though she seems to have been the earliest butt of his playfulness.

Because they were not very well off the Neri family did not live in the centre of the city but in the working-class suburb of San Giorgio which lies on the left bank of the river beneath the heights of San Miniato.

Philip was ever to be a lover of beautiful scenery, and every day his childlike eyes fed upon the sights of the enchanting city: the dome of Santa Maria del Fiore for example, beside Giotto's campanile; nearer, the lofty vigilant outline of the tower of the Signoria, flanked by the turret of the Palazzo del Bargello and the spire of Santa Croce; Mont Morello, the leader of the Apennine flock, standing out on the horizon; and down below, across the maze of gardens, the torrential yellow waters of the Arno hurling themselves under the arched bridges on which were perched a multitude of picturesque houses. It is impossible to describe the fresh, soft, penetrating radiance of the Tuscan scene which clothed everything with harmony and grace.

But 'the good Pippo' had only to leave his peaceful suburb of convents and market-gardens and cross the Ponte Vecchio to find himself in the City of the Red Lily surrounded by the splendour of Il Magnifico, for after the extraordinary interlude of Savonarola, the blissful life of the great Medicis—a life made up completely of music and poetry—appeared to have been revived in this city of beauty, while the springtime of Botticelli seemed to have returned.

The popular pastor Arlotto, who was a very good priest despite his buffoonery, and who hid a remarkably sensitive wisdom behind a jocular exterior, has sketched a brilliant picture of the joyous culture which had spread from the aristocrats of the *Orti Oricellair* to the most humble citizens.

All his life Philip was to dote on this man, and on the book in which his character and his sayings were to be immortalised for the Florentines. Did he not find in Arlotto his own brusque, spontaneous and gently facetious way of approach to persons and things which can co-exist with real holiness?

15

His best biographers have rightly recognised here his fundamental attitude to life, the earthly weft of his sanctity and its most Florentine quality.

But behind the façade of this faery and somewhat fantastic Florence the once blazing hearth of San Marco still smouldered. It was to show itself before long when the Medicis had again been expelled, when the city had come under the power of France and when the citizens strove to regain their liberty once and for all by reinstating Christ as King of Florence.

No one was more ready to share these hopes than the young Philip; his wonderfully bright clear eyes were as eager for the spectacle of the streets gaily decorated to welcome Pope Leo, as for the pure and tranquil paintings of the cloister where the memory of the spirit of Savonarola still blazed.

Much later he was to say to the Dominicans of the Minerva, 'Whatever good there is in me I owe to your Fathers of San Marco.'

Even the most pious of his biographers have been unable to hide the fact that he was a normal healthy child, untouched by any of those religious

16

crazes which sometimes divert even the naughtiest children. We must resign ourselves to the fact that 'Pippo' had no taste for building himself little altars and never expressed any intention of becoming a priest or monk. It does seem, however, that his one recorded flash of ill-temper is linked with an occasion when he and his sister Elizabeth were reciting the Psalms together and their small sister Catherine came to annoy them. All the purity of his childlike soul is revealed in the repentance which, so we are told, immediately followed his spontaneous reaction.

He was only just eighteen when he left his native city and there can be little doubt that it was the slenderness of the family's resources which drove him to travel some three hundred and seventy-five miles to try his luck with an uncle who had some money to leave.

The well-to-do Romolo welcomed him as a son to the little town of San Germano nestling in the shadow of Monte Cassino, hoping to hand on his business to him as soon as possible. Philip brought all his usual enthusiasm to this work but then something happened. It is unlikely that he had any misunderstanding with his uncle when we remember that he used to make a friend of everyone he met, but the fact remains that before very long he had given it all up, and taken the road to Rome to settle there for the rest of his life.

We shall never know exactly what influences were at work, but various explanations have been advanced. Perhaps he was influenced by the presence of that great Benedictine sanctuary on Monte Cassino, which overshadows the town; perhaps by his visits to the chapel of the Holy Trinity at Gaeta, suspended above the sea between cliffs riven, according to tradition, at the death of Christ.

Newman, writing of Philip's spirituality, certainly held that it owed a great deal to the Benedictines. From them he first acquired his love of the Scriptures, the Liturgy and the lives of the Desert Fathers, which were almost the only authorities he knew and which he drew on quite naturally. As to the shrine at Gaeta; it corresponds too well with his known taste for prayer where horizons were boundless, for us not to be tempted to associate it with his sudden change. Whatever the cause, Philip left for Rome after spending only a few months in San Germano, for he seems to have arrived towards the end of 1535 very soon after the departure of Benvenuto Cellini, to whom we are indebted for some idea of the sort of conditions prevailing there.

Some have maintained that the Renaissance died in 1527 with the sack of Rome by the Bourbon troops, a view certainly held by men like Michelangelo who despaired of any return to those enchanted days, and justified as we know now by future events, though it was certainly not the view of those who were young at the time; with all the irresponsibility of youth they sought to retain the former pattern.

The passion for antiquity and the dazzling springtime of art and poetry were certainly still alive and men's thoughts and passions knew no bounds.

In another sphere, however, the members of *The Oratory of Divine Love* were expending their enthusiasm on the incurables in their hospital at San Giacomo, while the Theatines, founded by St. Cajetan and Cardinal Caraffa, were at length winning the ears of a people disturbed if not made more wise by the catastrophe.

Above all, strange figures now appeared like apocalyptic warnings, in the midst of the pagan carnival which went on in spite of everything. There was Brandini, the famous hermit, foretelling more ruin and retribution for this modern Nineveh; Matteo da Boscio, the lay-brother from the Umbrian hills, seeking permission to return to the primitive Franciscan poverty, founding the Capuchins as if by accident; and Titelmans, the astonishing Dutch professor, who later joined Matteo da Boscio, petrifying the passers-by on the Ponte Sant'Angelo, where he had set up his pulpit, with his cries of 'Hell for sinners! Hell for adulterers!'

Nevertheless the countless Florentines attracted to Rome by the two Medici Popes Leo X and Clement VIII were still there and they had lost nothing of their frivolity; they had taken possession of a whole district in Rome on the left bank of the river, near the bridge which leads past Hadrian's Mausoleum to the Vatican. Their church standing on the banks of the Tiber was imposing yet unfinished, its colonnades which were to have extended out into the river, a fitting

20

symbol of their overweening pride which ended with the reign of the two Medicis.

In the studios of the jewellers, painters and sculptors, in the banks where usury flourished, was gathered a whole generation of intelligent, charming, impudent, spoilt young men. An entirely aesthetic culture like that of Florence could not be developed with impunity and Leo X, more clearly than anyone, understood its dangers. This new Epicurianism taught that a correct, if not irreproachable, moral life was no more than the final touch of elegance; surrender to the passions being repugnant to one who sought balance and harmony. Such a frail barrier might have been sufficient in a civilisation dying of its own refinement, in a civilisation where passions and restlessness of spirit had been dulled by the impoverishment of its stock and by inner decay; the case was entirely different now. A younger and more vigorous generation, captivated by beauty, freed from all control, and suspicious of any restraint, surrendered to the past and gave birth to a new paganism far more disturbing than the old. For these merely hereditary Christians, the magic of pagan pleasures were seen through a nostalgic veil, as of some lost Paradise. The grossest sin had but to clothe itself in beauty to be overlooked. The 'virtue' they sought was that so called by Machiavelli, the untiring energy to test every promise held out by the senses or the heart, 'to act, without considering whether the action be good or evil, to love without worrying if it be right or wrong'. How many Nathanaels proved themselves unable to resist such voices from the past, irresistibly fascinating because they had been silent for so long.

There is one tale of the time of Innocent VIII which shows how these Christians, out of touch with God, had kept the taste of the infinite on their lips ready to lend the illusion of it to any earthly food.

One day some masons found near the Appian Way the stone coffin of a young Roman girl bearing the simple inscription '*Julia Claudi Filia*'. When opened it revealed the incorrupt body of a young and lovely girl. The coffin and its contents were taken to the Capitol and the news of the exquisite yet macabre discovery flew round the city in a moment, to be followed by an almost incredible outburst of feeling; the body of the young girl seemed to attract the love and enthusiasm of every heart. From every quarter they flocked to assuage their imagined thirst for saintly beauty whose springtime lived for ever. The Pope, surprised and dismayed, was forced to have the body taken away secretly by night and buried beyond the Pincio.

As in these Romans of the fifteenth century, one finds in the young Florentines, whom Philip was to meet in the Eternal City a hundred years later, a paradoxical union of idealism and carnal passion, a languishing mysticism which can never be satisfied.

Laconic details from the notebooks of Leonardo, the equivocal smile he has given to some of his portraits, the burning sadness of Michelangelo's sonnets, all betray the disordered state of things in which the loftiest minds could be overcome by giddiness and fall like Benvenuto Cellini to disgusting depths.

What place has Philip in such a garden as this, where even the loveliest flowers smell of brimstone? The call from his peaceful retreat at San Germano to the turmoil of Rome was unquestionably a call to the apostolate.

On arriving there he set himself at once to win back the youth to Christ, but what weapons was he to use against the old pagan magic?

He did not seem attracted by any of the more ancient Orders; though he was still friendly with the Dominicans who had brought him up, he was no more likely to join them than he was to yield to the invitation of the monks of Monte Cassino. Nor did he feel drawn to the Capuchins, though Felix of Cantalice was one of his dearest friends. He sent so many recruits to the Jesuits that Ignatius roguishly called him 'The Society's Bell', calling others to enter while remaining outside himself.

The rigorous methods of the saintly Spaniard, says Newman, had the same effect on this free Florentine as Saul's armour had on David. He preferred to go forth to meet the subtle attractions of the new Paganism armed only with the more powerful attractions of purity and truth.

It was not that he condemned any method, old

or new; let those use them who made them; for
his part, he could never adapt himself to them;
he was too simple, too spontaneous, too direct,
perhaps even too lively, to place any armour
between himself and the world he planned to
conquer. Though this involved the loss of many
resources both in attack and defence, it did away
with anything which might have hindered direct
contact with the souls he sought; as it was, everyone could find immediate access to his mind and
heart.

His tactics were entirely spiritual and none
could avoid his influence except by avoiding him
altogether; and there he was, like another Socrates, with apparently nothing else to do but
wander about the Roman streets joining in every
kind of group quite freely, as ready to play quoits
as to pass his time in any shop where customers,
without any intention of buying anything, could
talk indefinitely. Far from being put out by
banter he soon earned a reputation for more than
holding his own; his presence attracted the gossips
and jokers who could be sure of entertainment in
his company, the vague fear of being told the

truth about themselves merely adding spice to the occasion.

This is not to imply that he hid his religion, but his very exhortations took the form of quips and his witticisms left a spark in the soul that did not die out easily. His shrewdness is shown by the fact that a teasing joke thrown out in passing often altered the whole course of someone's life.

The fact that a single word often helped a man to see himself as he was reveals his insight into the depths of the human soul. Some called him 'The Electric-eel'—an apt nickname—for contact with him electrified the most drowsy consciences; they would be roused from their lethargy as though by a shock and drawn by a magnetic force to join that happy band which could set off on a pilgrimage as if to a party.

It should be particularly noted that Philip neither taught any special doctrine nor any special devotions. He gave no orders, and asked nothing except perhaps by some pleasantry, the sense of which might not at first be apparent, yet no one could live in his company for any length of time without changing of their own free will.

26

If ever he did intervene it was to moderate their fervour rather than to arouse it—and he would do this in his own inimitable way. When, for example, the somewhat ostentatious Tarugi asked if he could wear a hairshirt he was told 'Certainly, as long as you wear it *over* your doublet.'

This unusual apostolate, depending for its effect on personal influence alone, on simple friendship in which a soul's whole life may be transformed, is typical of the Oratorian method, in so far as the Oratorian has any method. 'In the Oratory', says Bossuet, 'liberty and duty go hand in hand; one obeys without subservience, one governs without orders; all authority is rooted in gentleness, while mutual respect is maintained without recourse to fear; love, without any other yoke, is able to subdue and even annihilate self-will.'

Such an ideal, as Bossuet himself was aware, is not without its dangers. What, some may say, is this fine scheme really but that set out by Rabelais in his *Abbey of Thelema*, an earthly paradise? 'Their whole life was spent freely, according to their own desires and inclinations, without rules,

27

laws or statutes; their single precept: "*Do what you will*"; for those who are free, well born, well educated, those who move in the best circles, are always spurred on to do good and avoid evil by a natural instinct which they call Honour.'

Does not Philip, in fact, merely yield to Renaissance optimism? Does he not ignore original sin when he bases his apostolate on freedom and confidence? His 'religion without tears' surely expects from undisciplined nature what the discipline of grace alone can produce?

It would be useless to deny that it seems so; and it is here that the danger lies for the Oratorian, a danger arising from the ever-threatening confusion between a moral code based on human honour, and mysticism based on divine love.

Disciples frequently caricature their master and if this has happened in the case of Philip's disciples it is merely because they have not looked at the other side of the picture.

There is no doubt that it was dangerous to go out against the new paganism with no other arms save love, and just as dangerous to expose his apparently vulnerable simplicity to its disturbing influence, yet his outrageous method made him the victorious apostle of neo-pagan Rome. To understand this victory we must consider another side of his personality, and in doing so we come face to face with a disconcerting paradox. We must not in fact allow ourselves to be deceived; this man who spent the whole day in the streets led another life, concealed even from those who thought they knew everything about him.

To start with, what did he live on? Nothing, or almost nothing. Though he seemed to be a vagabond, he had nevertheless, as the result of a fortunate meeting, found a home on first reaching Rome, a home in which he remained as long as possible since it gave him the greatest possible freedom of movement, and because it gave him all he wanted: a position that just kept him from dying of hunger. His benefactor Galeotto Caccia, a Florentine, and head of the Roman customs, placed the education of his two sons, Michele and Ippolito, entirely in Philip's hands. It was a good start to his apostolate and the boys' parents would have enthusiastically endorsed the success of the experiment, but above all, it earned sufficient to satisfy his needs: a corner of the Customs-house to sleep in, a clothes-line for a wardrobe, and his food, a daily handful of corn and olives; all of which speaks volumes for his personal tastes!

The charwoman who used to watch him eating his ration every morning in the corner of the court-yard nearest to the well could have enlightened those learned critics who later described his spirituality as a mysticism without asceticism.

At the end of his life the last spiritual book he had read to him was *The Fathers of the Desert*, a book he always considered a manual of perfection; this may seem strange in the case of a man who was so sociable, but if anyone had followed him in the evening, after he had spent the whole day among young people without a moment to himself, and after his continual wanderings about the town had so wearied his limbs that they called out for rest, they would have been very puzzled.

Let us imagine the scene and follow him as he leaves his humble home with only a crust in his pocket and perhaps a book under his arm.

His steps lead him away from the Ponte Sant'Angelo; he circles the Forum and as night deepens, plunges into the deserted groves adjoining the Baths of Caracalla; darkness is almost complete as he passes out through the Porta San Paolo.

He is now outside the city; in complete silence and total darkness he stumbles along over the large paving stones, between the overhanging walls and beneath the laurels and cypresses of the Appian Way, until the moon picks out a dream-like silhouette ahead of him, the crenellated tomb of Caecilia Metella; there he turns to the right and finds himself almost at once in the deserted Basilica of San Sebastiano.

The church holds now no other presence save that guarded by the flickering flame. Alone with the Blessed Sacrament, Philip lingers in silent conversation.

The night is well advanced when at last he rises to his feet, though it is not the need for sleep that draws him away—there must be no mistake—this has been merely the beginning. He makes his way without hesitation through the familiar darkness to a flight of crumbling steps down which he plunges to an even darker night.

What draws him is not a mere crypt, but a secret kingdom which, led by an instinctive attraction, he has been one of the first to discover.

The steps lead to a network of galleries through which he passes as one who knows his way. The taper, lighted perhaps from the sanctuary lamp, serves to help him to re-discover cherished carvings and inscriptions, rather than to guide his feet; its light falls now upon the fish, now on the lamb and now upon the dove. And on the *loculi*, partitioned off like the cells of some huge hive in which eternal life awaits the burgeoning of everlasting spring, it lights these words constantly repeated in letters of the same dark red—'In Pace'.

This strange buried world still holds intact within its shrine of silent night and secret freshness, the early vanished life of Christian Rome. In this kingdom of the Dead, which his faith sees as a buried garden of God ready to burst out again in blossom upon the kingdom of the Living, Philip is as much, if not more, at home as in the sun-drenched streets where all we see is his gaiety.

Here, surrounded by the symbols of immortal life, he more than makes up for the sleep he has denied himself, by prayer in which the invisible world stands clearly revealed to his inward eye. He can no more dispense with this solitude thronged with spirits, a solitude denied him during the day, than could the monks of old whom he admired so much. Like them, he wishes to plunge himself, forgetful of time, deep into that absolute silence in which alone the Heart of God can speak to the heart of man.

His surprising freedom of spirit in the frivolous world, where so many others, even saints, dare not venture without a host of safeguards, springs from his strange familiarity with this hallowed world of the catacombs; when he leaves them all the clamour of the world is drowned for him in the echoes of eternity. Invigorated by his contact with the martyrs, his thirst quenched at the very source of Christianity, completely dead to the world so as to live in this world as though he were already in heaven, he is so completely centred on the world to come that this transitory world leaves him untouched.

It would be impossible to stress too much the importance of these two elements in Philip's life which can be explained only by the paradoxical combination of primitive asceticism and humanistic freedom. He was able to associate so intimately with others, and soften the hearts of the most godless of them, only because of the wealth of grace and love he derived from his deep interior life; he was able to mix freely with men enslaved by the world only because he could escape from it himself.

Later, it is true, he no longer visited this sepulchral retreat in search of solitude and silence but he found them again in the heights of his loggia at the Vallicella, and one might be tempted to see in this substitution the sign of a personal ascent; after the years of penance, in the darkness of night, his soul blossomed into the light of day. It would be mere supposition, however, for Philip never analysed his progress from the purgative to the unitive way, nor left us any means of doing so.

What cannot be doubted is the mysticism which crowned *all* his asceticism. This astonishingly human saint was saturated in the supernatural; this Florentine, while being truly a man of his times, seems to have stepped out of the Acts of the Apostles. Even the fire of Pentecost was for him a personal experience as we shall explain; certainly his astonishing serenity in the midst of the world can only be explained in the last analysis by the interior presence of an inextinguishable flame. This experience of the Holy Spirit's presence in his soul remains profoundly mysterious; it seems to have overflowed from his soul upon his body, foreshadowing the promised transfiguration of the resurrection. The heavenly fire seems, moreover, to have made itself felt through his heart to the extent of producing an inexplicable yet perceptible heat, while the marks of its presence remained within his breast, for it was revealed by the autopsy that the violent action of the heart had displaced two ribs. He described the experience briefly, on the eve of his death, to Consolini; it seems that about the year 1544, while praying in the catacombs, he had the vision of a ball of fire which entered his mouth and settled in his heart.

In the Litany composed in his honour by Newman we find an invocation which sums up everything, '*Cor flammigerum, ora pro nobis!*'

But to return to that earlier scene in the underground kingdom where we left Philip at prayer. Down a vent, half choked with weeds, a pale blue light has reached him, and a breath of air mingled with the scent of plants and earth, carries with it the freshness of morning. He rises to his feet and hastens out just as the last stars are fading from the sky; in the open it is still dark, but a crimson light is beginning to filter through the arches of the aqueduct of Claudius, casting fantastic patterns like fire on the Tomb of Caecilia Metella.

Farther on the houses on the Aventine begin to take shape, white against the trees of the great parks on the already sunlit hillside.

Philip knows that if he steps out briskly he will reach the church of San Girolamo just in time for Persiano Rosa's Mass.

II.—PRIEST

SUCH A LIFE IS SO UNUSUAL THAT WE ARE HARD
put to it to trace its subsequent course with any
accuracy, yet it did nevertheless have its anchor-
age; a church and a priest, neither in any way
ordinary.

In the very heart of Rome, San Girolamo della
Carita had until recently been a house of the
Franciscan Observants, who had then handed over
the house and the church as well, to the Pious
Confraternity of Charity.

Founded in 1518 by Cardinal Giulio de Medici,
on the pattern of a Florentine society of the same
name, it was well on the way to becoming the
largest charitable organisation not only in Rome
but in the whole of Italy.

At San Girolamo, moreover, in order to fulfil
conditions laid down by the Friars at the time of
the transfer, the Confraternity supported a community of priests whose sole task, though not an

easy one, was to serve the church. They occupied what had once been the dormitory of the monastery and was now partitioned off into small rooms. They had no superior, rank going by seniority. Those who undertook the regular services received a small stipend; those, on the other hand, who preferred not to bind themselves except for some occasional fixed service or hearing of confessions, were provided only with accommodation. Persiano Rosa, a modest and cheerful priest of humble stock, must have been one of the latter. Philip had met him by chance and had gone to confession to him; attracted by his goodness he had returned and a bond soon sprang up between them.

When Philip first met him he had a following of a dozen or so laymen, none of whom were people of note. They used to meet on Sundays and Feast days, go to Mass and Communion at San Girolamo and then adjourn to the priest's private room. There they would exchange ideas on the spiritual life with delightful simplicity, and Philip took a keen delight in the fervour and geniality of their meetings.

On the Feast of the Assumption, in 1548, Rosa, doubtless spurred on by Philip, proposed that the small group should be constituted a true Confraternity. When this came to the notice of the Cardinal Vicar Archinto, he urged them to combine some work of charity with their practices of personal piety, in particular suggesting that they should devote themselves to the care of pilgrims coming from the farthest corners of Europe; often penniless and more or less lost in this metropolis where they found everything so strange, these pilgrims certainly needed some one to look after them. Thus did the Trinita dei Pellegrini come to be founded and Philip became its moving spirit.

In the course of the Holy Year of 1550 the Congregation had developed to such an extent that they were able to give hospitality to five hundred pilgrims a day in the picturesque Ciambella, a property of Helena Orsini, situated near the Baths of Agrippa.

Let no one imagine that the Ciambella was anything like the present-day hostels provided for well-to-do pilgrims to Lourdes or Lisieux. It was more like a Salvation Army hostel, and the pilgrims themselves, their devotion having made them vagabonds, resembled tramps rather than the devout tourists whom we call pilgrims today. Philip and his companions gave themselves wholeheartedly to the task of bathing their feet, clothing them, feeding them, and nursing them when they fell sick.

Such charitable works, however, were not allowed to usurp the place of the spiritual exercises and devout conversations which were still held to be of prime importance.

After several moves they arranged to carry out their charitable work in San Salvatore in Monte, until in 1563 they moved finally to San Benedetto in Arenula, specially assigned to them for their meetings by Pius IV. In the meanwhile their work had attracted considerable attention.

In 1551, for example, they had introduced the new devotion of the Forty Hours at the beginning of each month. In the presence of the Blessed Sacrament exposed they took it in turn to maintain continuous prayer interspersed with *fervorini*. Philip naturally excelled in delivering these fervent discourses, and, seeing him display such varied gifts, an idea occurred to Persiano Rosa. After some hesitation, because it seemed strange that Philip had not thought of it himself, he at last spoke: 'Why don't you become a priest?'

With perfect candour Philip admitted that he had never considered the matter. Though this was largely due to humility it transpired further that the thought of joining any ready-made organisation was distasteful to him.

Persiano Rosa answered Philip's objections by making him admit that his own priestly duties at San Girolamo left him completely free. As willing to accept the advice of a trusted counsellor as to express his own views, he allowed himself to be persuaded.

He had already followed a more or less regular course of theological studies for his own satisfaction during the years when he was wandering about; besides, no one enquired very closely into such things in those days. As we have already mentioned, Persiano Rosa was a friend of the Cardinal Vicar of Rome and the latter left to him the final preparation of this candidate for the priesthood. Once the matter was decided there was no delay. Within six months Philip had received all his Orders; ordained deacon on Holy Saturday in the Lateran, he received the priesthood on the 23rd May 1551 at San Tomaso in Parione.

Now that he was a priest the 'Reverendo Messer Filippo' could no longer in common decency spend his nights as before between the Customs-house and the catacombs or under the portico of some basilica.

He moved to one of the rooms in San Girolamo and became so fond of his tiny cell overlooking the narrow cloister lined with orange trees, that it required the express order of the Pope himself to make him leave it, and this was after thirty-two years. Only then as founder and, despite himself, superior, did he move to live with the congregation which he had brought into being almost unconsciously.

In the meanwhile what was his new life at San Girolamo to be like? From the very first he was to be engrossed in the two great functions of a priest—the hearing of confessions and the cele-bration of Mass.

Today this does not appear so very unusual; its originality will be better appreciated when we realise that the practice of frequent confession and communion was almost unheard of; nor did those in Holy Orders celebrate Mass every day as they do now.

San Girolamo had been remarkable, ever since the time of the Franciscans, for the many services held there every day, and the first duty of the chaplains who replaced the friars was to ensure their regular celebration.

Philip was always very careful, however, to avoid accepting any payment that would make him responsible for regular duties, though this did not prevent him from adopting a regular routine in the use of his time.

Except on rare occasions he spent every morn-ing in church hearing confessions, until about noon, when he ended his long period of duty by celebrating the last Mass of the day.

At first, although busy in the confessional, there were occasional slack periods, which he spent saying the Office or the Rosary or in reading and meditation. Soon, however, these periods became shorter and less frequent.

Who were all the people who flocked to his confessional? The majority were young men, and it is not hard to guess who were the first to come: all those he had met in the course of his wanderings and conversations in the city, those who had seen him at work among the sick at the Trinita dei Pellegrini, or heard him speak during the Forty Hours.

It must be added that when he settled down at San Girolamo he had come in contact with another devout group, where his influence at once found a fresh field of operation.

The atmosphere at San Girolamo was entirely different from that in which his apostolate had hitherto been exercised.

The outstanding originality of the place sprang from the almost complete independence enjoyed by the priests there so that each of them worked in an entirely personal sphere, beginning any new enterprise that appealed to him and gathering about him his individual disciples; San Giro-

lamo was in fact a regular colony of small assem-
blies each with its own meeting place in one of the
Fathers' rooms.

The strangest of these groups and the group
which Philip joined from the start, centred
around Buonsignore Cacciaguerra, a sick priest,
old before his time, whose story reminds us of
the *Arabian Nights*.

A native of Siena, born at the end of the
fifteenth century of a family of powerful mer-
chants, he had gone to Palermo and set up in
business there.

Having become fabulously rich he dazzled the
people of Sicily by a mode of life oriental in
its refinement of luxury and pleasure.

From time to time there would be a break in
these Bacchanalia. Cacciaguerra would dismiss his
friends, disband his harem, put away his extravagant and princely clothes and give up perfumes,
music and dancing . . . he was going to make his
Easter duties, or his conscience had been pricked
by the sight of a beggar. In the latter case he
would bring the man into his own palatial home,
tearfully tend him and serve him at his own table.

The next day, however, would see him back again with his current mistress.

But once, hurrying back to his interrupted pleasure, the sound of a strange stumbling step behind him made him look round, and what did he see? Christ carrying His cross. From then on he suffered one catastrophe after another, one after another his ships foundered; one of his amorous intrigues which turned out badly, left him disfigured by many dagger scars; his even more remarkable misfortunes are best passed over.

After pilgrimages of penance all over Europe, each a romantic adventure, he returned to Palermo to find that he had been robbed by his brother of all he had left. His mouth eaten away by a running sore, he was taken in by an old negress who had once been one of his slaves.

For a time he lived there in solitude, then retired to the mountains only to return unexpectedly, leaving behind him in the towns through which he passed, a trail of miraculous cures. Once more he travelled all over Europe, this time a lay apostle of daily communion.

Finally in 1547, while temporarily in Rome, he

was ordained priest, and in 1550 joined the community at San Girolamo, becoming at once the centre of a group of fervent devotees.

Two ideas and two ideas only animated his followers: daily communion and reparation for sin by voluntary suffering, all in a blinding atmosphere of ecstasies and visions.

Philip was enthralled no doubt by the sombre gravity and real generosity of their mysticism, but what seems to have appealed to him particularly was Cacciaguerra's idea that frequent communion should be regarded as the means of leading a more perfect Christian life rather than its term, and he kept his head in this company where common-sense was not always given its due place.

Cacciaguerra's ecstatic penitents were going to be given mortifications of a new kind by Philip: ludicrous remarks, quite unmerciful practical jokes and well-timed humiliations at the height of their ecstasies became the order of the day. A great and much needed gust of fresh air came in with Philip, but none seem to have held it against him, which says something at any rate in favour of their over-zealous spirituality.

For several years the two groups that gravitated about Cacciaguerra and Philip, though not absolutely identical, were barely distinguishable.

When away from Rome the disciples of one wrote just as readily to the other, and when the members of the Confraternity of Charity began to worry about their chaplains' innovations, the little war was waged against both priests together.

They had to endure many uncomfortable months, even years, though the persecution did not go much beyond the annoying behaviour of the sacristans and the personal animosity of Teccosi, the President of the Confraternity.

Philip, for example, who detested everything dirty and whose concentration at the altar soon became well known, found his Mass impeded in all sorts of ways, and only dared approach the altar clothed in the shabbiest vestments that were in the sacristy.

In the end, however, his patience triumphed over every prejudice; as for Cacciaguerra, he always came out of these skirmishes victorious, and when in 1558 the house was reorganised and a superior at last appointed, it was he who was given the post.

It seems, however, that this final victory was the signal for his retirement; henceforward he devoted himself to an ever-diminishing group which cultivated an ever-increasing esoteric mysticism, leaving Philip with an undivided influence and a clear field.

From this moment, in fact, Philip became the focal point of something which could not as yet be called an institution but which, without need of any rule, had achieved a true regularity.

From the young men who came to make their confessions to him, Philip quickly picked out those who could give God more than the minimum service and he never found it hard to get them to come back sometime in the afternoon when they were free. So it was that they formed the habit of gathering daily in his room before going out for the customary Roman saunter in the cool of the evening.

At first, on account of the smallness of the room, the number must have been fairly small, not more than seven or eight; nor could anything be less formal than these meetings. Half reclining on the bed Philip would talk as man to man, though sometimes when he was rather tired, or afraid of going into an ecstasy if he spoke of God, he would ask someone else to start the ball rolling.

At first it seems he spoke in the same simple way as had been the custom at Persiano Rosa's, but soon he had to adapt his material to a more educated class of people, to minds more lively and brilliant. He would use a book, perhaps one of the Gospels, St. John for preference, or the writings of some mystic, though he was always careful to avoid mere speculation, as such, or anything which his young audience might find unreal. After reading a few pages he would put the book away and his explanation of what had been read would lead quite naturally to an exhortation, though he preferred to encourage immediate discussion by asking a sudden question. In either case he tried to avoid doing all the talking and encouraged the group to work things out for themselves. The evening's stroll in no way interrupted their talks, rather the opposite. They went usually to one of the great Basilicas; if they had only a little time to spare, St. John Lateran or Santa Croce was their most obvious choice unless, crossing the Tiber at once, they went to say their prayers beneath the half-finished dome of St. Peter's. It was not easy to tear themselves away from anyone so charming as Philip and so when he returned home at night-fall most of the group would come back with him to San Girolamo. His room would be by now in darkness, he would light a single little lamp and all would kneel; depending on the need of the moment they would join in spontaneous prayer —Philip finding it easy to inspire his young followers with something of his own fervour.

The popularity of his afternoon gatherings soon compelled him to use the room next door as well, until even this proved insufficient. The next move was to a loft in the church, which had once been a granary, and one of Cacciaguerra's first acts on becoming superior was to assign this officially to Philip for his meetings. This new meeting-place, which came to be called the Oratory, gave its name to the exercises held there and later to the Congregation which sprang from them.

This extension of his work compelled Philip to abandon something of its original spontaneity; mere conversation was no longer sufficient and so Philip would invite one or another of the small nucleus of his disciples to prepare an address, always expecting that it would be concrete, and never allowing it to become a scholastic or academic discourse. Later, when the Oratory as such was founded and there was a church to look after, everyone had to preach, though Philip insisted on the utmost simplicity; one disciple who offended in this matter was compelled to repeat his excessively polished sermon seven times in succession! What appealed to Philip most of all, however, was his original 'talk on the book', as it came to be called, and it is interesting to notice the texts he was accustomed to use: most of them were taken from early spiritual writers such as Cassian or John Climacus, or from some of the greatest writers of the Middle Ages, Gerson, Denys the Carthusian, Richard of St. Victor, or St. Catherine of Siena. Any of the lives of the saints were popular but Philip seems to have shown a marked preference for the lives of the Desert Fathers, and with his inimitable humour once said to Gallonio, who came across him reading them again for his own benefit, 'I'm reading the story of old men like myself!'

Philip had brought with him from Florence two contemporary books which give us some idea of the atmosphere of the original Oratory. One of them was the *Life of Blessed Colombini*, in which it is safe to say he saw the ideal he wished to convey to his followers: to have Christ and His love always on one's lips, because one had them always in one's heart, yet to see Christian charity as the best sermon of all, then finally, to attain true detachment through generous self-denial.

The other book was the *Laudi* of Jacopone de Todi. In these Umbrian poems of the late thirteenth century we find afresh the Franciscan teaching on poverty, not perhaps with the utterly dazzling joy of St. Francis's *Song of Brother Sun*, but with a lyrical outburst of repentance which casts the heart, overwhelmed by faith and love, at the feet of Christ crucified.

Philip, avoiding the slightest didactic tendency, enlivened the discussion on such books with amusing or profoundly spiritual remarks which were always practical. He liked the conversations to be interspersed with music and the meetings to be brought to a close by some singing, so that the evening was filled with harmony.

The programme of their meetings took some ten years to crystallise into the following form: reading with commentary, the commentary taking the form of a conversation, followed by an exhortation by some other speaker. This would be followed in turn by a talk on Church History, with finally, another reading with a commentary, this time from the life of some saint. All this was interspersed with short prayers, hymns and music, and the service always finished with the singing of a new motet or anthem. It was taken for granted that everyone could come and go as they chose, as Philip himself did. He and the other speakers used to sit quite informally on a slightly raised bench facing the gathering.

We have already compared one of Philip's activities to those of the Salvation Army; the same comparison holds good for these informal meetings.

Generally speaking, the pattern followed by Evangelist meetings, invented as is supposed by Anglo-Saxon revivalists of the eighteenth century, was no more than a repetition of this Roman priest's experiment in the sixteenth century. We find the same spontaneity, jealously suspicious of any rule which might bridle inspiration or lead to formalism, the same outburst of sensible fervour, above all the same attempt to return to the Gospels and make them available to everyone; while over all there reigned a fragrance, a delicate touch, an indefinable something, drawn from the pure air of the Tuscan sky.

In all truth nothing but one of Animuccia's lovely motets could distil the essence of the Oratory and pass it on undiluted.

With certain reservations there is much in common between those earlier evening meetings and those of Methodists and Quakers today; the long minutes of silent prayer in common, spiritual reading and more or less impromptu prayers.

It was at such prayer meetings as these,

intended it is true for the more fervent, yet excluding none, that Philip asked someone to read aloud some recently published letters from Jesuit missionaries in the Far East. These letters aroused in Philip and his followers the dream of setting off together to seek martyrdom in India.

One day in the course of a walk they consulted the Superior of San Paolo fuori de Mura who suggested that they should ask the advice of a Cistercian monk at Tre Fontane. His reply, more or less inspired, became a watch-word for the group. 'Your India is here in Rome.' On Sundays and particularly on Feast days after Vespers at San Girolamo, Philip used to wait for his friends outside the church; the party would form quickly and set off in high spirits, ever growing as it went on its way. Where were they going? Anywhere. In those days there was little need to go beyond the town for an outing. Whether they went off in the direction of the Baths of Diocletian or in the opposite direction over the slopes of the Janiculum, they could find magnificent ruins in the midst of fresh and lovely flowers and trees with the restful murmur of fountains never far away. They used to sit down under the spreading trees and their open-air meeting would be more than usually entertaining and artistic.

On such occasions music played a more important part than ever. Animuccia would bring along Rome's best musicians, and the 'Adoramus te Christe' by Orlando de Lassus, or the 'O vos omnes' by Vittoria, would mingle with the sound of the fountains' silvery cascades, of the leaves rustling in the sea breeze.

They followed no rigid programme. With Philip the unexpected was the rule; a visit to a hospital on the way was just as likely as some extravagant practical joke—usually at the expense of the great Baronius.

On long summer afternoons they often went beyond the city to visit Tre Fontane, as we have already mentioned, or Frascati, or Tivoli, but their favourite long walk, and incidentally the most beautiful, was their pilgrimage to the Seven Basilicas.

It was a long way and it was their recognised custom to cross the Tiber to St. Peter's the evening before to pray at the confessional encircled by its

golden cluster of flickering lamps, setting off next
morning in twos and threes along the Via Ostia to
St. Paul's.

In that vast country basilica, its great walls
lashed by the surge of wheat fields, they would
reassemble, then set off across country along the
Via Ardeatina to San Sebastiano which for Philip
held such cherished memories.

On their way in the freshness of those early
summer mornings on the Roman Campagna,
Serafino Razzi's *Laudi* would alternate with
Gregorian Litanies.

At San Sebastiano those who had not already
been to confession went now, and then would
follow a fine Polyphonic Mass, perhaps Palestrina's wonderful 'Mass of Pope Marcellus' or his
'Ecce Sacerdos magnus'. All who had come so far
without breaking their fast went to Communion,
then off they would set again singing along the
Appian Way. Before returning to the city they
might invade a vineyard like that of the Crescenzi
not far from the Pyramid of Caius Cestius,
scattering among the shady places and enjoying
a well-earned meal together, the same for every-

one: fresh bread, some of the famous Roman 'salami' with an egg, some fruit and a glass of local wine. They set off again before the heat became too oppressive to reach the shade of the Lateran before the sun was at its height. If some of them dozed off during the sermon there they were quickly roused by the hymns which followed. On leaving they never failed to climb the nearby Scala Santa, on their knees, a reminder that a pilgrimage, however merry it may be, was still an ascetic exercise.

It was little more than a stone's throw from there to Santa Croce and then they had only to follow Hadrian's Wall to San Lorenzo. Beneath the peaceful shade of the tall cypress trees alongside the vast necropolis, this Roman deacon's shrine would be the scene of a final meditation.

On their return to the centre of the city they would visit Santa Maria Maggiore on the heights of the Esquiline. Beneath the ceiling which Alexander VI had just had decorated with the first American gold to be brought by Christopher Columbus from Peru, and among the Ionic columns of pure white marble, the day would draw to a close in an outburst of Palestrina music, and a 'Salve Regina' would fill the falling night with its loveliness gathered from the rivers and the stars.

The time has come now to look more closely at Philip's recruits.

There is material enough for a whole gallery of extraordinarily varied portraits; the only thing they seem to have in common, apart from youth, is generosity of heart concealed beneath that sparkling gaiety which is, as it were, the hall-mark of a Philippino.

The fraternity, prepared as it was to ignore all distinctions of rank and position, included among those who flocked to Philip's room, noble-men, musicians or singers from the basilicas, small tradesmen, young Jews lured from the Ghetto by Philip's charm, bishops' servants and even highway robbers in addition to the original apprentices and employees from the Florentine banks. Philip behaved in the same way to them all, yet never seems to have hesitated over what would suit each one.

60

As, for example, he wanders about the room waiting for Oratory to begin, he may notice the shoemaker from next door sitting timidly on one of the benches at the back; he goes to him at once and shows him the greatest consideration.

Why does he stay hidden away in this poky corner when he should be sitting in the front row? Despite a stream of excuses, Philip takes hold of him by the collar, leads him to the front, and by the sheer force of his friendly banter, puts him at his ease. This good fellowship, naturally enough, shows itself rather differently in the case of a person of rank, someone, for example, like Gian Battista Salviati, a cousin of the Queen of France. Yet it is this same friend-liness, as prompt to tenderness as to irony, that wins him over from the start.

Robbers were mentioned as being among the company. One day as he was looking round the room for new faces, Philip noticed someone who was obviously a jail-bird. He must have wondered how on earth he came to be there but he welcomed him as though he had been a long-lost friend. Taken unawares, the stranger was somewhat unresponsive at first, but he surrendered like the rest and before long went up to Philip's room and made his confession as simply as a child.

As there is neither time nor space to describe everyone, we will single out two, both belonging to the innermost circle of his disciples, certainly with little else in common.

First, Tarugi, Papal Chamberlain, a cousin of Julius III and Marcellus II, a close friend of Cardinal Ranuccio Farnese, and the grandson of Paul III, he had all the distinction of a man of the world. As famous for his good looks as for his exquisite manners, a past-master in every sport, a fine soldier and an intrepid leader, he had inherited every artistic and literary gift from his great-uncle, Angelo Poliziano, just as he had inherited the jurist's impartial mind from his father. His friendship with Cardinal Innocenzo di Monte, that well-known 'Viveur', is enough to explain how, at the age of thirty, his reputation was very far from good, though he was not entirely without better feelings. He began to go to confession to Philip from time to time and the charm worked all by itself, so well, in fact, that Philip had great difficulty in preventing him from becoming a Capuchin. Seeing clearly that this brilliant young man needed a thorough grounding in humility before embarking on any religious life, he preferred to make him walk by his side through the streets wearing his velvet suit and carrying Capriccio in his arms, Capriccio being Cardinal Ascanio Sforza's dog which became attached to Philip and to Philip's room.

As soon as such trials as this had had their effect, Tarugi became quite a spoilt child of Philip's, though that did not mean that Philip, in his politely ironical way, asked less of him than he asked of the others, rather the contrary.

Caesar Baronius, the second of Philip's disciples to become a Cardinal, was cast in a very different mould. A rough diamond from the mountains of Abruzzi, he had come to Rome in 1557 and his family had made every sacrifice possible to enable him to continue the studies he had begun at Naples.

A friend of his took him along to Philip's where he too fell under his spell. With his unshakable good sense, his ox-like application to his work, his patience, his dog-like fidelity—even though it was the fidelity of a growling dog—the 'Barbarian', as Philip used to call him, gladdened the saint's heart more than words can tell, and became his privileged butt.

At the Oratory, Tarugi captivated everyone with his natural eloquence and was never at a loss, no matter what the topic of the moment might be. Baronius, on the other hand, desperately serious, could speak on one topic alone; whatever his subject he always worked round to describing the sufferings of hell with such a wealth of detail that it made everyone's flesh creep. To keep him off this subject Philip made him speak on the history of the Church. Obediently, Caesar studied his subject deeply; his great learning, sense of duty and application bore fruit in his valuable *Annales Ecclesiastici*.

When they had both become members of the Sacred College, Tarugi distinguished himself as much by his political genius as by his spirituality. Baronius remained to the end an unspoilt countryman, but his homespun honesty earned him no less esteem than the astonishing political successes of his colleague.

Cardinal de Joyeuse has left us with a very endearing sketch of him in a letter to the French King, Henry IV. His sympathies with the French were well known and in the Conclave of 1605, the French Cardinals fixed their choice upon this devout and learned disciple of Philip; but they had not allowed either for his scrupulous conscience or for his stubbornness. Pushed this way and that towards the Pauline Chapel for a vote by acclamation, the 'Barbarian' clung desperately to the posts and carvings of the doors as he shouted, 'I don't want to be Pope, choose someone worthy of the Holy See.' These things, however, belong to the far-off future. Before becoming Cardinals, Baronius and Tarugi had first to join the Oratory and we still have to tell how Philip himself unintentionally brought this about.

III.—SAINT

PHILIP WAS RAISED TO THE PRIESTHOOD DURING
the Pontificate of Julius III, a sort of St. Martin's
summer of the Renaissance.

The Council of Trent continued, but without
much enthusiasm, and the Carnival, with all its
follies, had started again in Rome; yet the great
schemes for Catholic reform had begun at last
and were being put into operation. In particular,
it was during these years that the Society of Jesus
became firmly established and made its prepar-
ations for rapid expansion.

However, in 1555, everything changed with
the accession to the Papal Throne of the awe-
inspiring Caraffa; for the first time the Curia
itself became the subject of reform. Paul III had
been content to promote to the Curia a few of the
more illustrious Christian humanists, such as Con-
tarini, Jacopo Sadoleto, or Reginald Pole. Paul IV
set out to force even such as were already mem-

bers to change their ways completely, or break them like glass.

He warned the aged Cardinal du Bellay, the senior Cardinal, that he would have to set the example. 'That', said the Cardinal ironically, 'is to entrust the key of the wine cellar to the biggest drinker', an observation worthy of the patron of François Rabelais.

The laughter did not last very long. Arrest and banishment of high prelates grew frequent and, to crown all, the Pope's anti-Spanish policy led Italy into another war and brought her to the very brink of fresh disaster.

Such events made many people think seriously and the Oratory suddenly expanded with an influx of converts.

Meanwhile, in 1558, further clouds were forming. It seemed that Paul IV, who was preparing the first edition of the *Index Librorum Prohibitorum* planned to include the works of Savonarola.

Philip, with his truly Florentine devotion to the prophet of San Marco, was of one mind with the Dominicans of Santa Maria sopra Minerva, and their joint prayers managed to avert the threat; but the atmosphere became oppressive the following year when the crimes and peculations of even his own family became the object of the reforming Pope's energetic wrath.

How could any institution as independent as the Oratory avoid attracting unwelcome attention when it had to live in the very shadow of this unprecedented spiritual dictatorship the very agents of which were the first to fall under suspicion?

In Lent the pilgrimage to the Seven Basilicas was forbidden and Philip was ordered to appear before the Cardinal Vicar Rosario, who was even more of an inquisitor than the Pope himself. However, within a few days of the dramatic interview in which Philip found himself and his work the objects of the most dire threats, Rosario died suddenly on his way to a Papal audience. The Pope relented and cancelled the measures already taken, but within a few months he too died. When on the 19th August that year a revengeful mob overturned the statue of the late Pope in the Capitol, Philip, incapable of bearing a grudge, could not restrain his tears.

Under Pius IV everyone was able to breathe freely again, but during the great reforming pontificate of St. Pius V the Oratory was to suffer further setbacks. The counter-reformation was already under way; nothing, it must be admitted, was less indicative of the state of siege in which the church found herself than Philip's work, but certainly it aimed at reform in its own way.

Several times the Pope ordered investigations and several times Philip felt himself directly threatened, so much that he seems to have considered a move, perhaps to Milan, where another saint called for his collaboration.

On every occasion, however, powerful supporters intervened, in particular Cardinal Borromeo, and in the end the storm dispersed without breaking.

From the accession of Pope Gregory XIII Philip had no more to fear, while Gregory XIV and Clement VIII were more than protectors, they were intimate friends; by that time, however, Philip was not only accepted by everyone as the new apostle of Rome, he was being treated as a patriarch. His flourishing congregation would have developed into a great order had not his determined opposition prevented it.

How had this come about? To all appearances in a most fortuitous manner.

In 1564 the Florentines, from the colony of the Red Lily, sent what was virtually a formal deputation to ask him if he would accept the position of Rector of San Giovanni, the half-finished church standing on the banks of the Tiber.

Philip, just recovering from a serious illness, declared that nothing would induce him to leave San Girolamo, or to consider for a moment abandoning the Oratory which was his life's work. At the same time he did not want to disappoint his beloved fellow-citizens and a solution suggested itself: he appointed several of his most trusted disciples to act as chaplains there under his more or less nominal supervision.

The fact that none of them were priests as yet, constituted no difficulty. Baronius needed hardly any preparation before being ordained, and two others, Bordini and Fedeli, soon followed.

From every point of view the solution appears

to have been providential. True they had to walk from San Girolamo to San Giovanni and back every day, but to Philip's companions walking was no hardship.

The congregation of the Oratory had come into being; though it would take another year or so for anyone to realise it, the decisive step had been taken.

The new chaplains were sons of Philip; that single link was enough to ensure that they lived in the most intimate union of thought and feeling, while the priesthood served to bring them even closer.

Further, the spirit of Philip nourished in them a priestly spirituality which he had unconsciously formed and himself already exemplified in his own life.

They had no intention, moreover, of becoming 'regulars', having, like Philip himself, no desire to be anything more than a secular priest should be. They wished simply to be priests of the Oratory, that is, priests who preached, in the words of one of his disciples, 'the daily and familiar word of God'. This remark may seem

71

trifling, but in fact it says everything, for the distinctive mark of Philip's preaching was precisely that highly personal manner in which he carried it out—a form of preaching that had nothing conventional about it; to establish direct communication with his hearers the more natural it was the better.

Cardinal Newman's motto, '*Cor ad cor loquitur*', sums up the Philippian ideal; neither speeches nor arguments can awaken a living faith in those for whom Christianity has lost its meaning. Only contact with people whose daily lives are dominated by an intense and personal experience of the truths of the Faith can achieve such a result, and it is precisely this result which Philip achieved through his dual life of intimate communion with God and men.

The Oratory was nothing more than the spontaneous development of this principle in the conditions offered by sixteenth-century Rome, its methods capable of being altered when different circumstances demanded a different expression of the same simple, vital principle.

Meanwhile, the Florentines, wishing to please

their new chaplains, gave them the ancient church of Sant'Orsola della Pieta, almost opposite San Giovanni. It was soon obvious, however, that they could not carry on the work of the Oratory and at the same time look after a large parish, so in 1575 they moved to the little church of Santa Maria della Vallicella.

It was a decisive step, for the Papal Bull authorising this move gave the Oratory canonical recognition, expressly stating that in this church was established in perpetuity 'a Congregation of secular priests called the Oratory'.

The expression 'a Congregation of secular priests', seemingly a contradiction in terms, was unprecedented, while the use of the term 'The Oratory' legally transferred to the society the name originally attached to its exercises.

However, as this is a study of Philip rather than of the Oratory, these details are enough, nor shall we say anything here about the foundations that sprang up in Naples and elsewhere. The Roman Oratory housed in Santa Maria della Vallicella which was, after all, little better than a ruin, concentrated its energies on building the

E*

magnificent Chiesa Nuova. They began this task
with little or no capital but fortunately they were
able to use the foundations of an ancient wall
and the work was quickly completed with the
help of generous benefactors, the most prominent
of whom was Cardinal Cesi.

In 1583, as we have mentioned, Philip was
persuaded, through the personal intervention of
the Pope, to leave San Girolamo and live with
his Congregation. He got his own back on those
who had forced his hand by organising a mock
triumphal march. He made his disciples cross the
city, under a hail of jibes, carrying, each one, a
single piece of Philip's shabby furniture. Although
he was one of the most respected religious
leaders in Rome he had not become in the least
pompous. To the intense relief of Tarugi, Capriccio
had died a long time ago, and so did not have to
be carried. It is true that Capriccio had been succeeded by a cat, but she, like many of her kind
more attached to places than to people, refused to
leave San Girolamo. However, Gallonio, one of the
more recent recruits to the Oratory, was sent every
day to make sure that she got her bowl of milk.

Philip continued to exercise a fascination over youth. After Gallonio, whom Philip used to tease all day long, there came the brilliant Juvenal Ancina; the future Bishop of Saluzzo, and a friend of St. Francis de Sales, he was destined himself for Beatification. Then there came Consolini, the Benjamin of the family. Philip was by now an old man and his powers were rapidly declining, though he could still hold his own and his voice was as clear as ever. It was the most difficult thing in the world to persuade him to take a little rest, delegate some of his duties or add something to a diet which made that of a Trappist, by comparison, seem positively festive. His only concession was to hear confessions in his room instead of in the church. He still went out at all hours to wander round the city, the same as ever, his wit just as keen, his heart as warm. As time went on, however, he began to keep more and more to his two little rooms at the top of the house at the Vallicella, and passed endless hours in the even smaller loggia beneath the roof. It is a mystery how he could spend so long there in winter without freezing to death. Solitude gradually claimed

him more and more; true he received all who
called on him and turned no one away, yet
the Holy Spirit was slowly becoming his sole
companion.

His absorption with the invisible world was
clearly manifested in the extraordinary Masses
which he celebrated in one of his two rooms. At
the 'Domine non sum dignus' the server used to
close the shutters, put out the candles and replace
them by a small lamp. He would then leave,
after pinning a notice on the door, 'Silence, the
father is saying Mass'; when he returned two
hours later Philip would still be wrapt in the daily
ecstasy of his communion.

One after another persons of the highest rank
came to visit him, joining company with the
youth of Rome and Florence. Charles Borromeo,
Cardinal Frederic Borromeo and many other prelates were frequent visitors to the little upstairs
room. One of them, Cardinal Vallier, wrote a
dialogue after the manner of Plato, entitled
'Philip or Christian Joy' and was the first to call
him, so aptly, 'The Christian Socrates'.

In the spring of 1594 he was forced to take to

his bed. All Rome was alarmed and the Pope anxiously awaited the latest news of him. Relapse succeeded recovery until, with everyone on the brink of despair, he was cured by a vision of Our Lady.

The following spring he fell ill again and this time his case was considered hopeless, though he himself was quite sure that he would be able to say Mass on his Feast day, 1st May.

He did in fact do so and was apparently cured, but it was not long before he was again seized by violent attacks of fever, brought on by his chronic catarrh.

On the 12th of May he had a hæmorrhage, and Baronius gave him Extreme Unction. Cardinal Borromeo thought at first that he was too weak to receive Viaticum, but finally he decided to bring it to him, and Philip began to improve as soon as he saw the host, saying, his voice as strong as ever, 'Behold My Love, give Him to me at once.' As the Cardinal repeated the 'Domine non sum dignus', Philip, in tears, was saying, 'I have never done anything good, not a thing.' A few days later, to the amazement of his doctors, he was up and about again and had not seemed in such good health for a long time. The good news soon spread but he himself was not deceived. When Consolini said, in his hearing, that there was no need to say any more Masses for him, he interposed, 'On the contrary, say a black Mass for me. I know how I am.'

He spent the morning of 25th May, his favourite Feast of Corpus Christi, hearing confessions and then celebrated his last Mass. He had several visitors, including Cardinal Cusano, who recited Office with him. In the evening he had his usual light supper and went to bed. When their work was at an end, the Fathers came for his Blessing and he asked what time it was. Someone told him that it was about eleven o'clock. No one paid any particular attention when he repeated, as if mechanically, 'Three hours, three hours.' But at two o'clock in the morning, Gallonio, who occupied the room below, heard Philip tapping with his stick on the floor. He ran upstairs to find him sitting on the bed breathing with difficulty. At once he sent for the doctor, but Philip simply said, 'It's all over, I'm dying.' Meanwhile the

Fathers had been gathering in his room, and Baronius said the prayers for the dying. When he had finished, he said to Philip, 'You're not going to leave us, Father, without giving us your blessing?' Philip, who had remained seated on the bed all this time, opened his eyes for a moment and sighed, then his head fell forward, and his earthly life was over.

His body, laid out in the Vallicella, became immediately a centre of pilgrimage for the whole of Rome, though he was not to be Beatified until 1615. On 12th March 1622, in company with Ignatius Loyola, Francis Xavier and Teresa of Avila, he was canonised by Gregory XV.

EPILOGUE

How, in cold words, can we capture the spirit of Philip or explain the charm this hunter of souls exercised over his prey?

There can be no doubt that what first attracted people to Philip was the manifest presence of the Holy Spirit in his soul. Not everyone experienced it in the same way, but no one who spent any length of time in his company was in any doubt about it. The manifestations of this presence were sometimes extraordinary. For example, he often felt a burning sensation within his breast and even in the depths of winter he had to leave his windows open to keep cool, a fact which explains how he endured his long watches in the ice-cold loggia of the Vallicella. This feeling was not merely subjective, for countless witnesses testified to having felt the heat of this internal flame, when, as often happened, he pressed a penitent's head to his heart. Temptations would be dispelled, a troubled mind set at peace, a conscience purified by contact with this mysterious fire.

On other occasions he found himself unable to say the Our Father without going into an ecstasy. In fact, a single thought was often enough, as on the occasion when one of his disciples entered his room one morning and found him obviously overtaken by an ecstasy as he was dressing himself. Naturally enough Philip wanted at all costs to avoid such revealing manifestations and was almost at his wits' end to find a remedy. In the sacristy, before Mass, he used to divert himself with dogs or birds, and even went so far as to have his favourite book of jokes read to him. At the altar, when he felt an ecstasy coming on, he sometimes walked backwards and forwards along the altar steps, speaking to his server. Sometimes he would toy with his keys or his watch while he read the Gospel. But it was not much help; as he proceeded with the Sacrifice he would be seized by an ecstasy over which he had no control. Sometimes he sang, rather than recited the words, sometimes he was seen to rise from the floor after the Consecration, until, finally, as already mentioned, he had to say Mass in private.

It is not surprising, therefore, that in his later years he gave up speaking in public, for after a few words he would be unable to go on.

On one occasion he had to leave the pulpit before he had said anything, muttering to himself, as he came down the steps, 'Those who ask for ecstasies don't know what they are asking for.' None of this, it may be admitted, was necessarily supernatural and, separated from their context, such phenomena might be interpreted as no more than pathological symptoms; but the presence of the Holy Spirit was betrayed in other and more certain ways, for example, in his gift of clairvoyance. Certain examples, such as being able to forecast what Pope would be elected, might be attributed to natural causes. What is not so easily explained, is the way in which, without hesitation, he could give his penitents a detailed list of their shortcomings, even their most secret thoughts, as soon as they knelt before him. If any of them expressed astonishment, he would pass the matter off with a joke, as in the case of the bearded young man, who asked him, 'What was it, Father, that helped you to know my sins?' 'Your downy beard,' answered Philip.

How, for example, can we explain his suddenly leaving his confessional on one occasion to stop someone he had seen crossing the church and who, a moment later, was pouring out a sad story known to him and God alone . . . but which Philip had whispered in his ear. Such things were of almost daily occurrence, and were so well known that one of his younger disciples, when tempted to sin, was able to resist by merely saying to himself, 'No, Father Philip would know at once.'

Few saints have lived more naturally amid the supernatural or combined with their mysticism so much practical common sense. None, for example, judged unusual phenomena more objectively than he himself; always on guard against every possible delusion, he gave little credence to reports of extraordinary favours. When, for example, someone was telling him about the 'mystical sickness' of a certain devout woman, his immediate reply was, 'It is time she got married.' He was delighted on being told by a woman who had seen him rise from the floor while saying Mass, that she thought he must be possessed; he laughed, saying, 'It is quite true, I am possessed.'

We find united in him a most virile purity and a most compassionate tenderness. Few saints have been able to share the pains and pleasures of others, to weep and rejoice with them as much as Philip, and no other saint seems to have been so ready to manifest his feelings: his tears and laughter flowing from a deep personal sincerity which made him one with all men.

His extravagant behaviour cannot be passed over without some explanation. Why, for example, when certain Polish noblemen came to visit him at the Vallicella, seeking edification, did he have read aloud the most ridiculous passages from pastor Arlotto saying that it was his spiritual reading? Why, when invited to the house of one of his penitents, a rich Roman lady who had invited him to meet her worldly relatives, did he arrive with half his beard shaved off? Why, when some scholarly Bishop, little given to jesting, attended his Mass, did he commit every possible error in pronunciation? Why did he sometimes wear a red jersey or a fur coat over his cassock? Why did he walk through the streets carrying a bouquet of flowers in his hand, or perform a burlesque dance before an audience of Cardinals chanting comic verses which he made up as he went along?

Was it merely to make a fool of himself and cause others to think little of him?

His buffoonery cannot be so simply explained, for we must take into consideration the pranks he was constantly playing on others. These pranks took many forms; some were merely unexpected and ludicrous, as when he pulled the impressive beard of a Swiss Guard, others were more elaborate, as when he sent Baronius to a wineshop to sample all the wines before buying half a bottle; to make it all the worse he had to offer a gold piece in payment and ask for change. Then there was the somewhat scandalous prank he used to play on people who came to him for miraculous cures. He would give them a small sachet which they were to place on the affected part, with the proviso that they must *on no account* open it. As soon as he died the recipients could restrain their curiosity no longer. On opening up their sachets they found that they contained nothing more than a cheap holy medal!

Certainly Philip acted in this way to lower himself in the eyes of the world yet there are many saints who would have found it difficult even to understand anyone using such strange methods of doing so. Most of his biographers try to explain or excuse them, but not very convincingly. A more direct approach is necessary.

Philip indulged in these jests primarily because he had a natural tendency that way and saw it as no part of his duty to resist a tendency which was not fundamentally evil. There was more to it than that of course. The almost systematic way in which he developed his buffoonery had an ulterior motive and his biographers are certainly right in drawing attention to this, provided that they do not restrict their explanation to this point alone. Philip did not exaggerate his eccentricities simply in order to pass as an addle-pate; his unbounded humour was the spontaneous expression of that freedom which to him was inseparable from being in a state of grace, the freedom of the children of God.

He knew that the Devil is ever striving to make us take grace for granted, claim it as a right or place ourselves on an equality with God and that is why he continually prevented those about him from taking themselves too seriously.

The only antidote to the deadly seriousness into which pride can lead us is, when all is said and done, the joyful simplicity of the children of God. Why should children in their Father's arms be other than joyful? They alone in the world have the secret of true freedom and happiness, and even if those who cannot fathom the reason for their joy, judge it madness, they can, with a clear conscience, make their own the words of *Wisdom*:

'*I was at His side . . . my delight increasing with every day, as I made play before Him all the while, made play in this world of dust, with the sons of Adam for my play-fellows.*'[1]

[1]*Proverbs* viii. 31.

87

CHRONOLOGY

1515   Born in Florence on 21 July.

1533   Goes to his uncle Romolo in San Germano.

1535   Travels to Rome where he lives a life of prayer and study and begins a lay apostolate.

1548   Founds the Confraternity of the Holy Trinity for the sanctification of its own members and the care of pilgrims, with Fr Persiano Rosa his spiritual director.

1551   Ordained priest on 23 May and goes to live at St Girolomo della Carità. He begins to give conferences in his room, the origin of the 'Oratory'.

1575   Pope Gregory XIII gives the community the Church of Santa Maria in Vallicella, which St Philip rebuilds and which becomes known as the Chiesa Nuova (New Church). The congregation of the Oratory is approved by the Pope on 15 July.

1595   St Philip dies on 26 May.

1622   Canonised (with St Ignatius and St Teresa of Avila).

CARDINAL NEWMAN'S PRAYER
TO ST PHILIP

PHILIP, my glorious advocate, teach me to look at all I see around me after thy pattern as the creatures of God. Let me never forget that the same God who made me, made the whole world and all men and all animals that are in it. Gain me the grace to love all God's works for God's sake, and all men for the sake of my Lord and Saviour who has redeemed them by the Cross. And especially let me be tender and compassionate and loving towards all Christians, as my brethren in grace. And do thou, who on earth wast so tender to all, be especially tender to us, and feel for us, bear with us in all our troubles, and gain for us from God, with whom thou dwellest in beatific light, all the aids necessary for bringing us safely to Him and to thee.

(from *Meditations and Devotions*)

CPSIA information can be obtained at www.ICGtesting.com
Printed in the USA
LVOW08s0000171113

361613LV00001B/53/P